# Bikini Babes

## Hot Sexy Bikini Girls
## Models Pictures

### By **PHOTO ART LOVER**

### Copyright © Bikini Babes

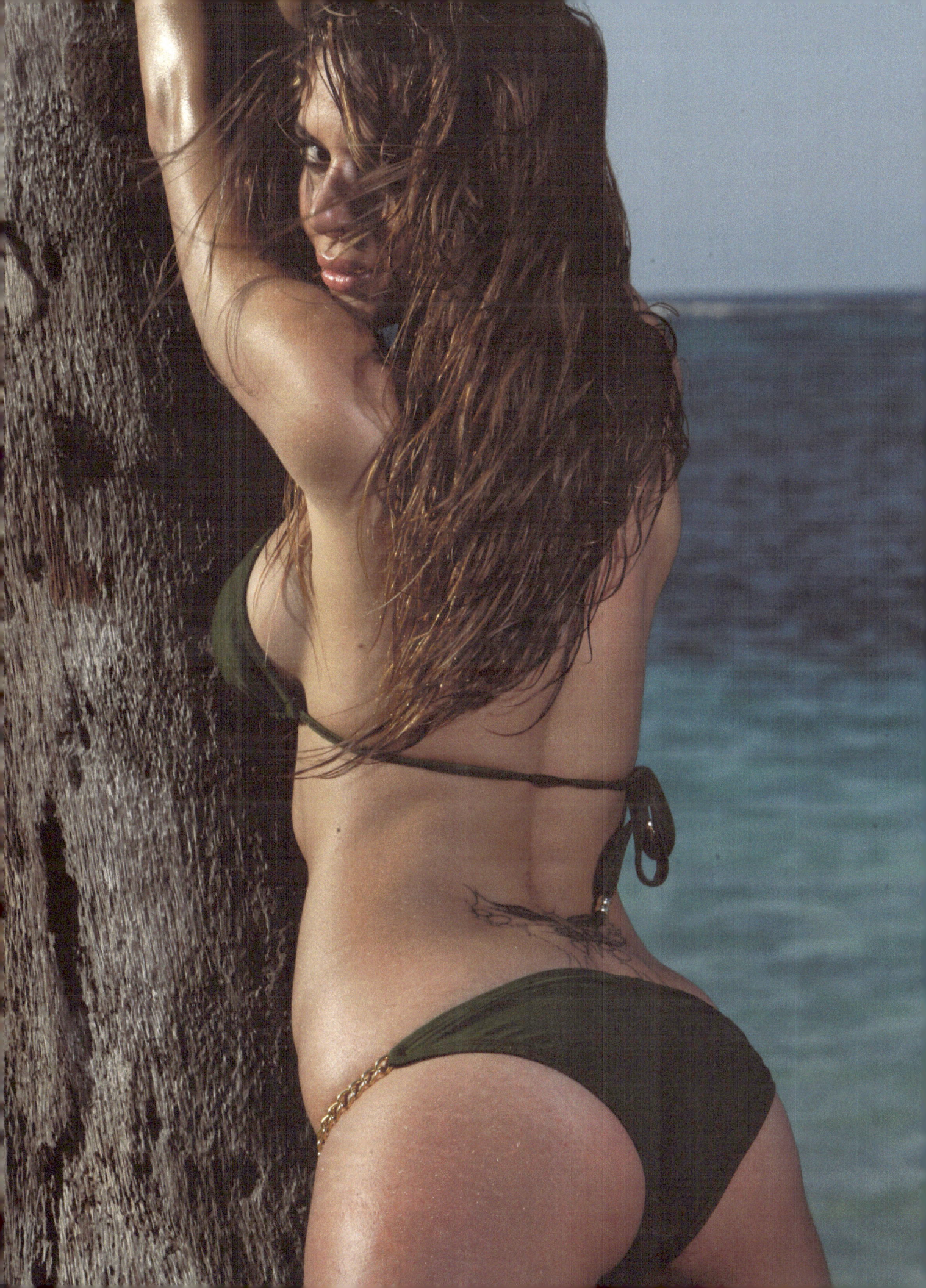

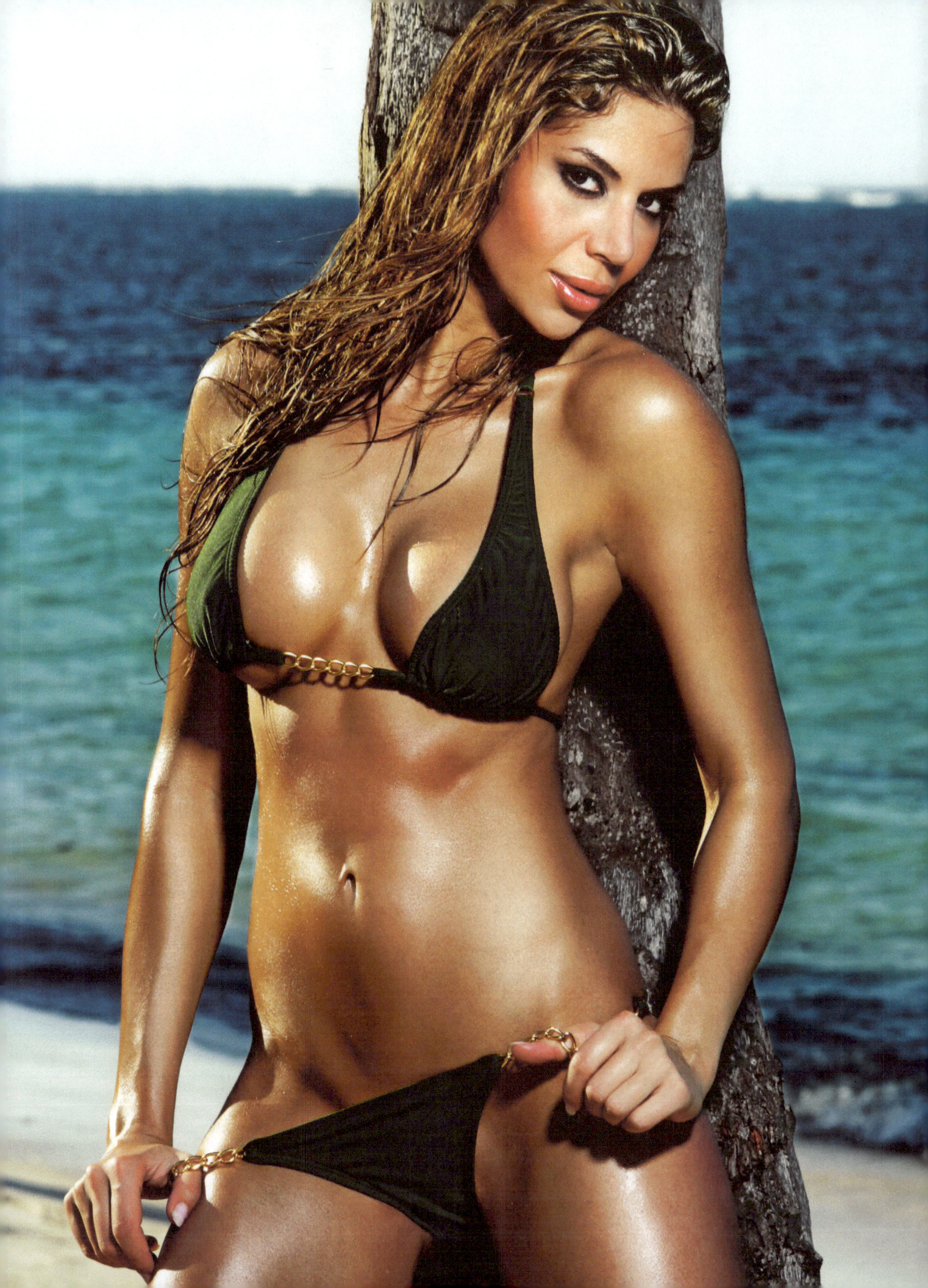

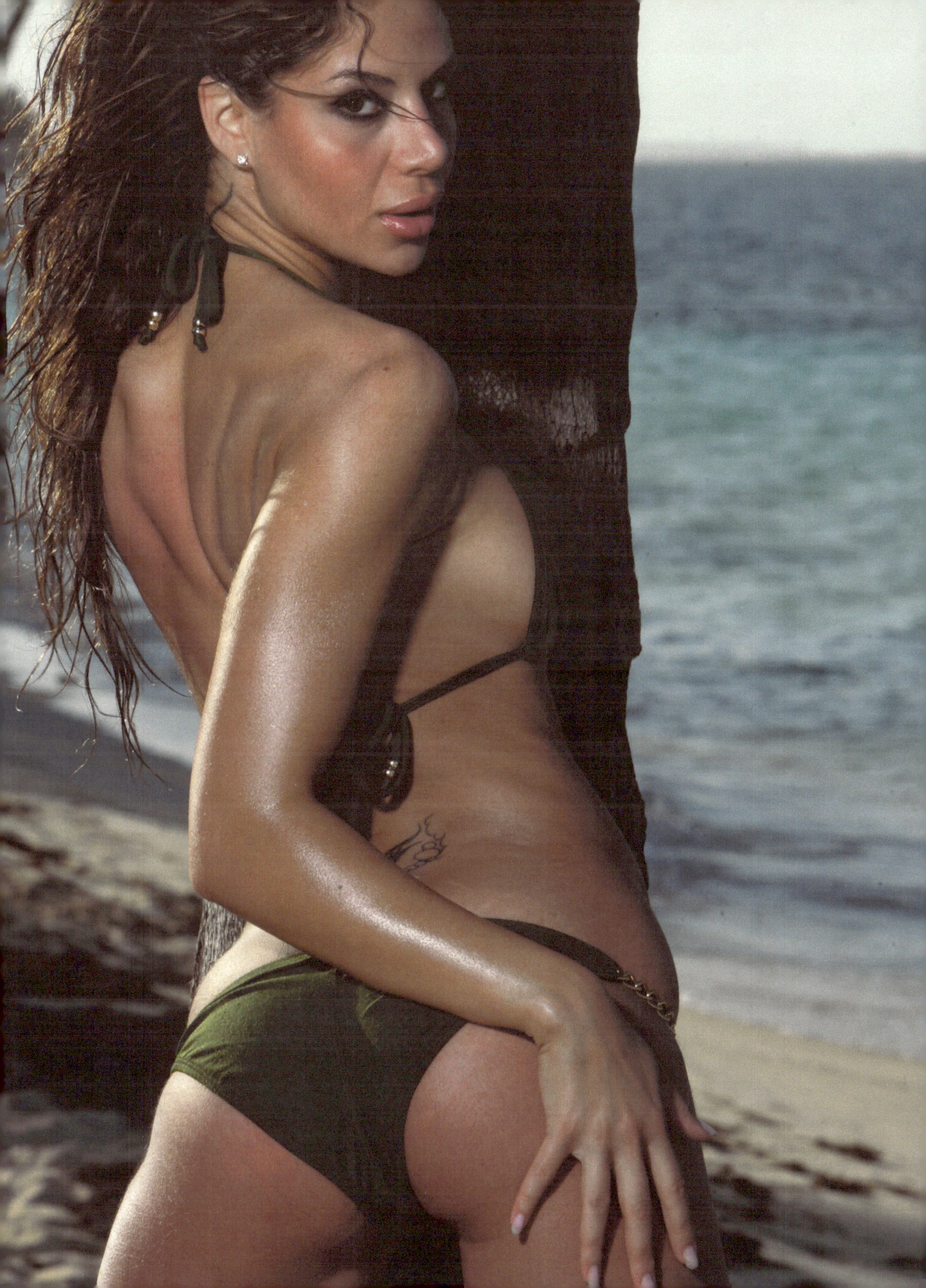

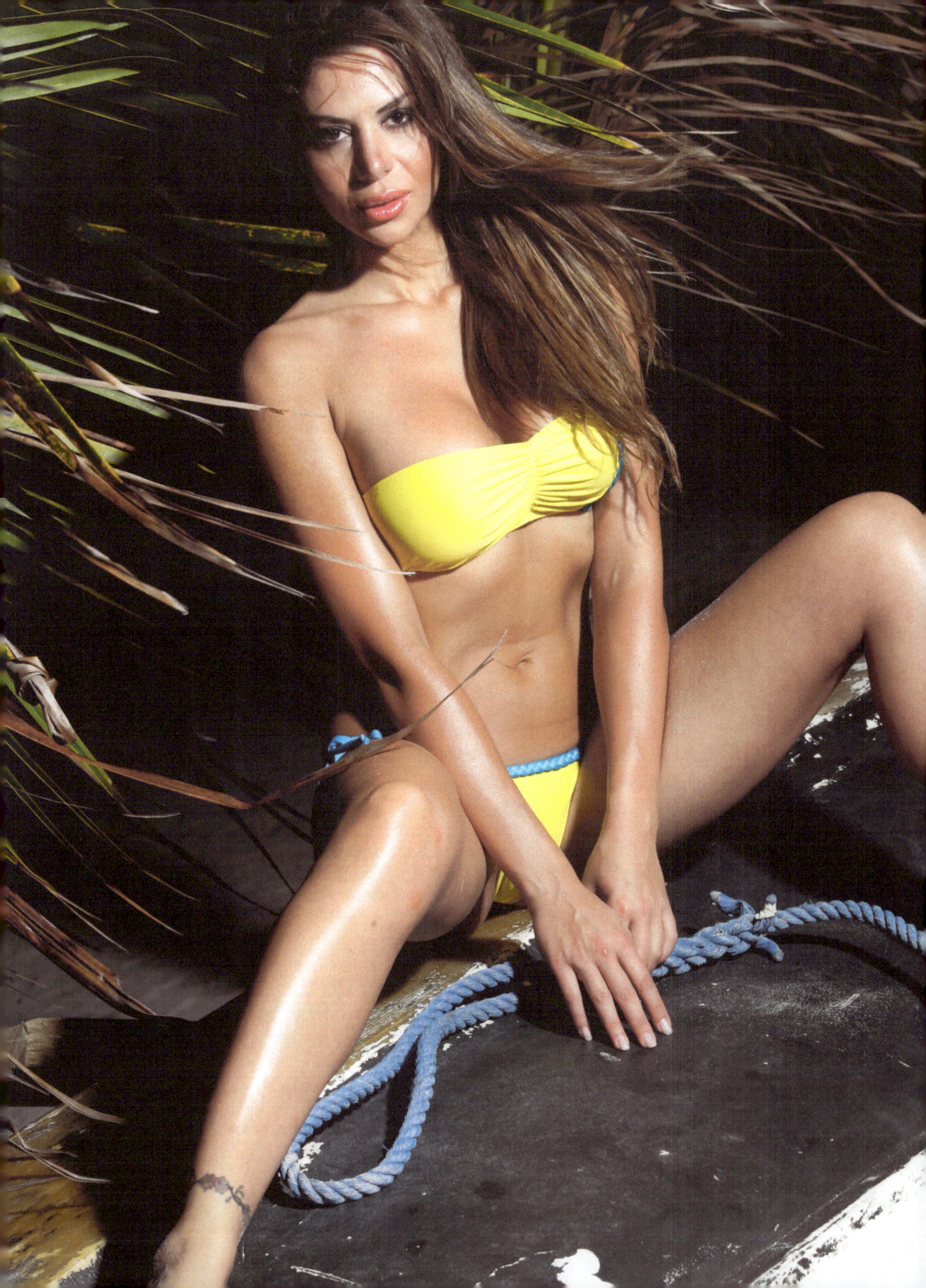

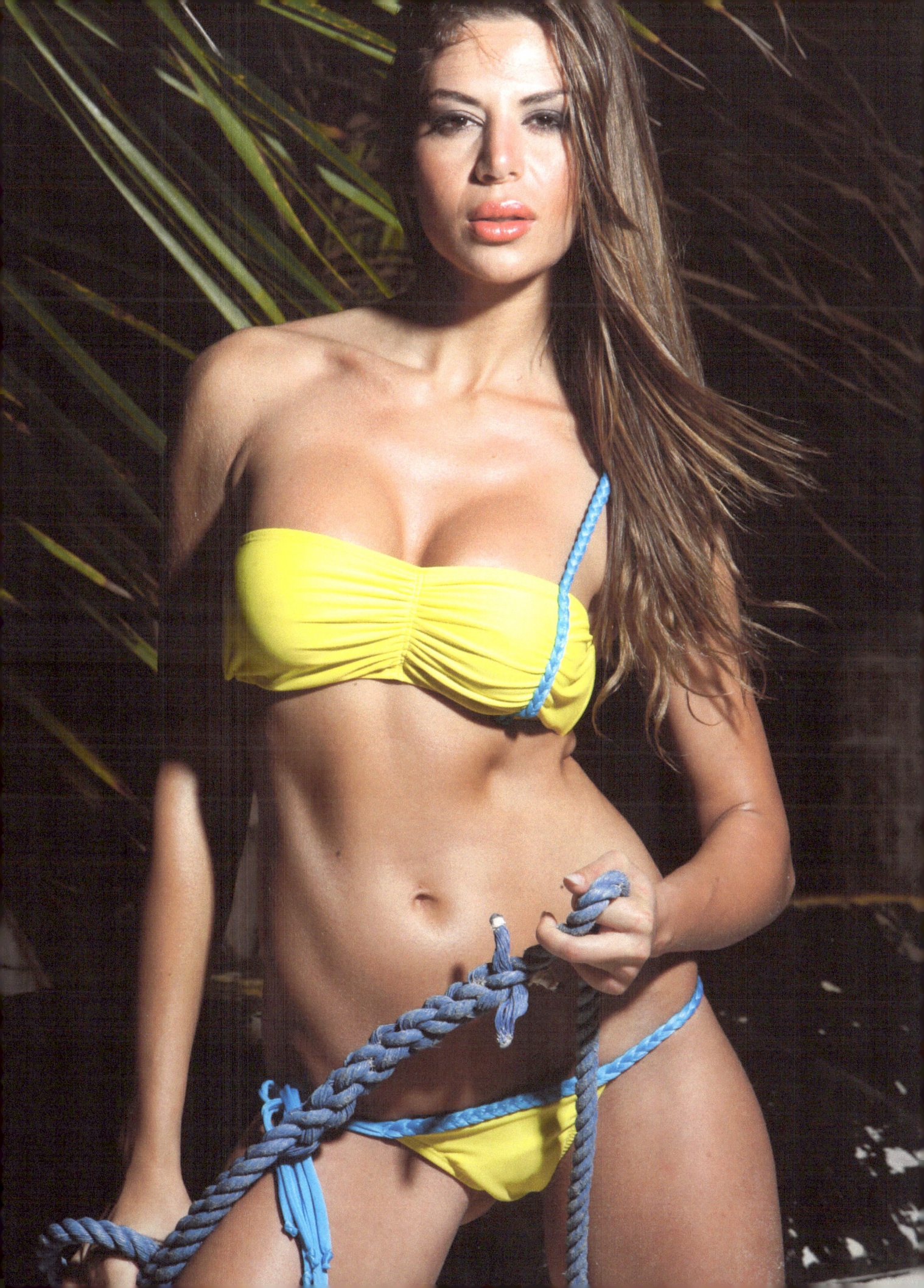

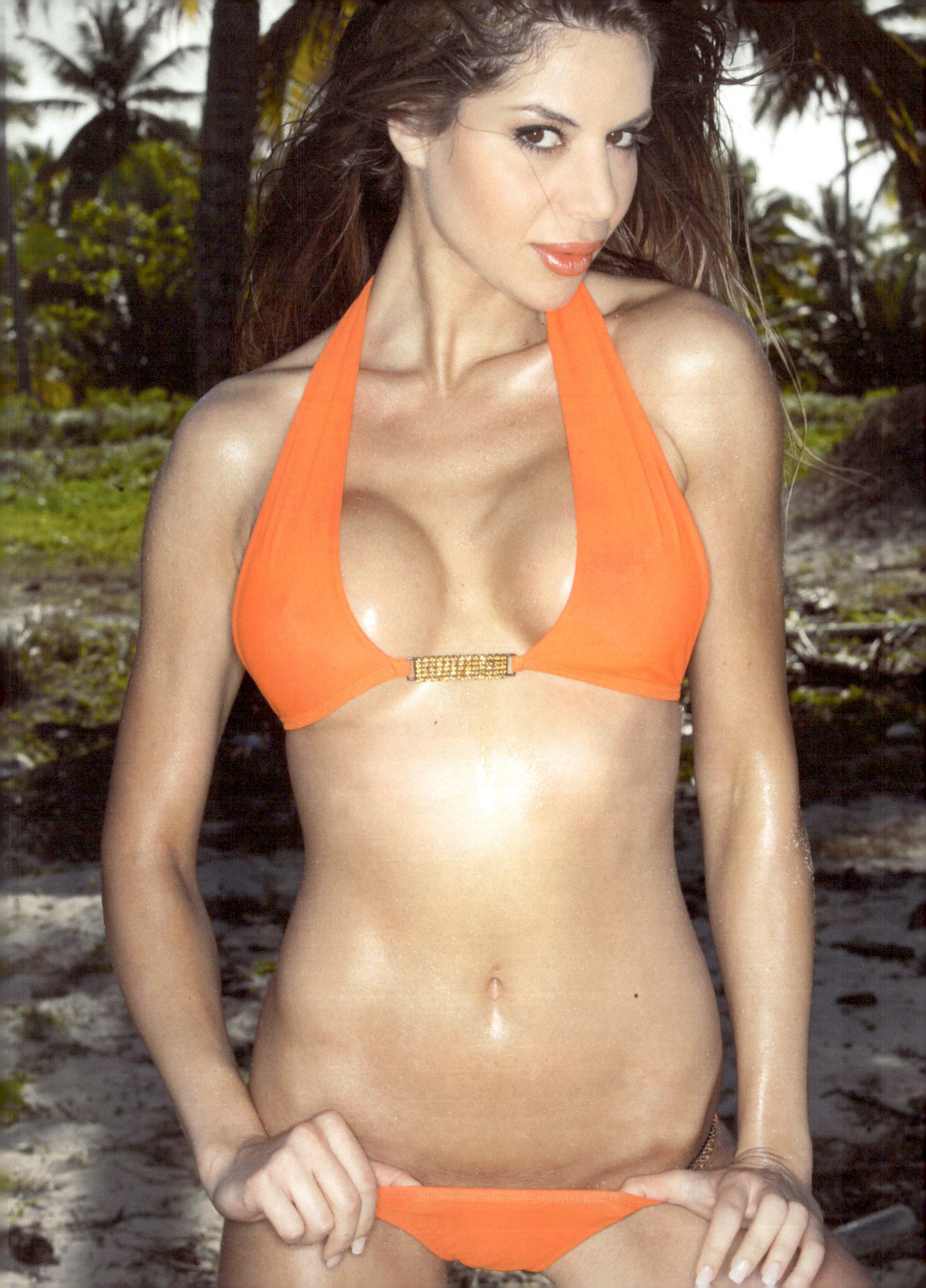

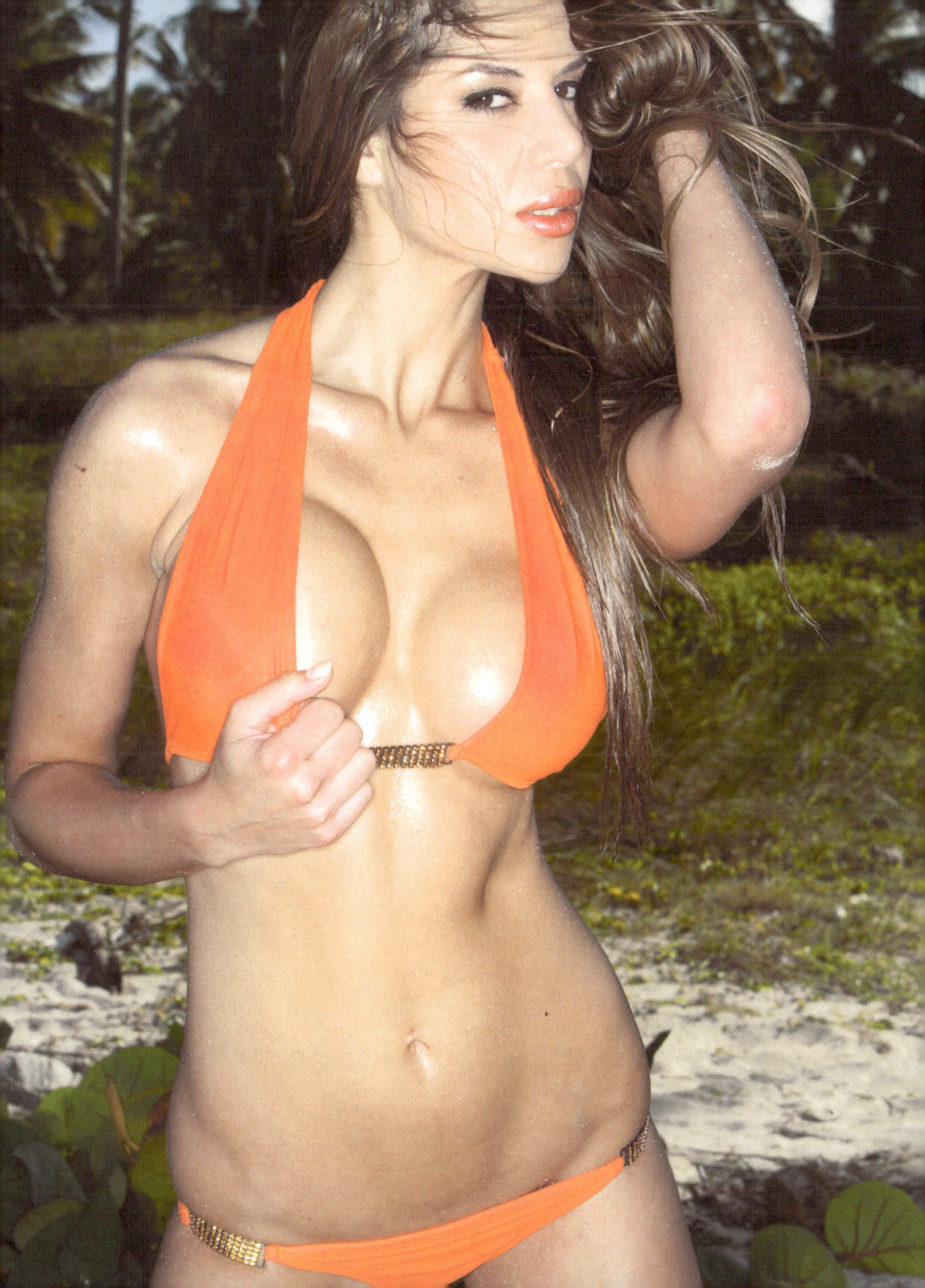

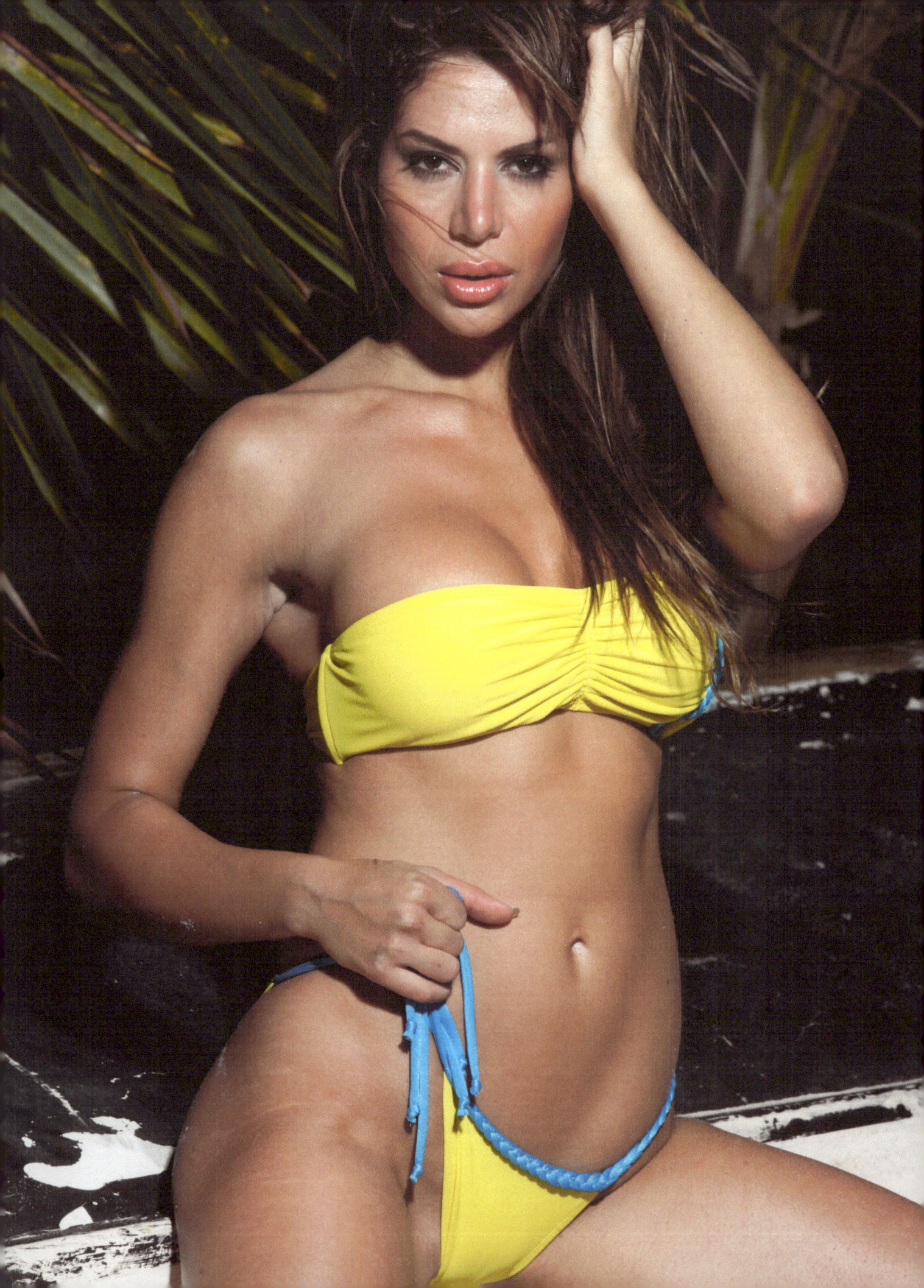

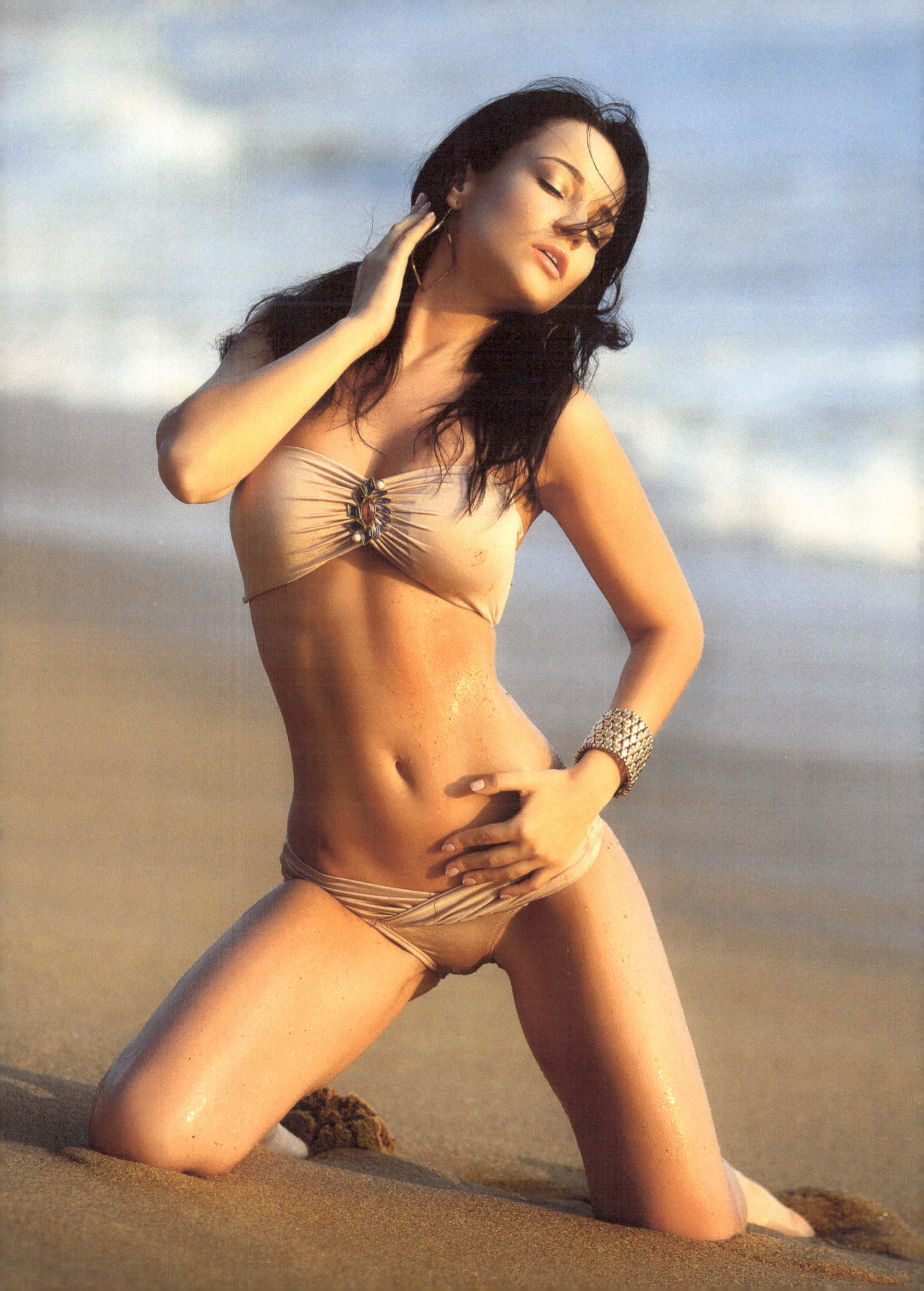

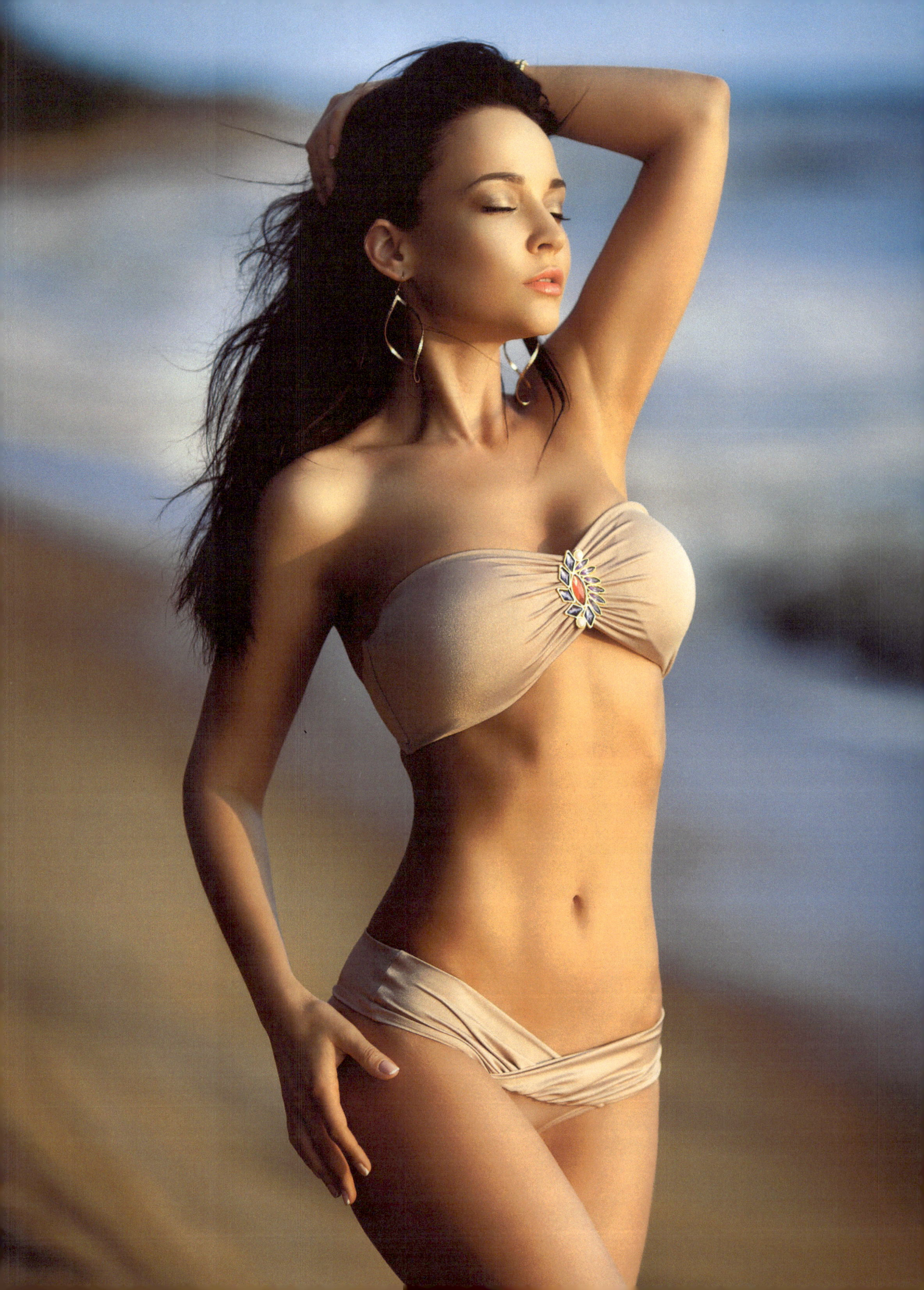

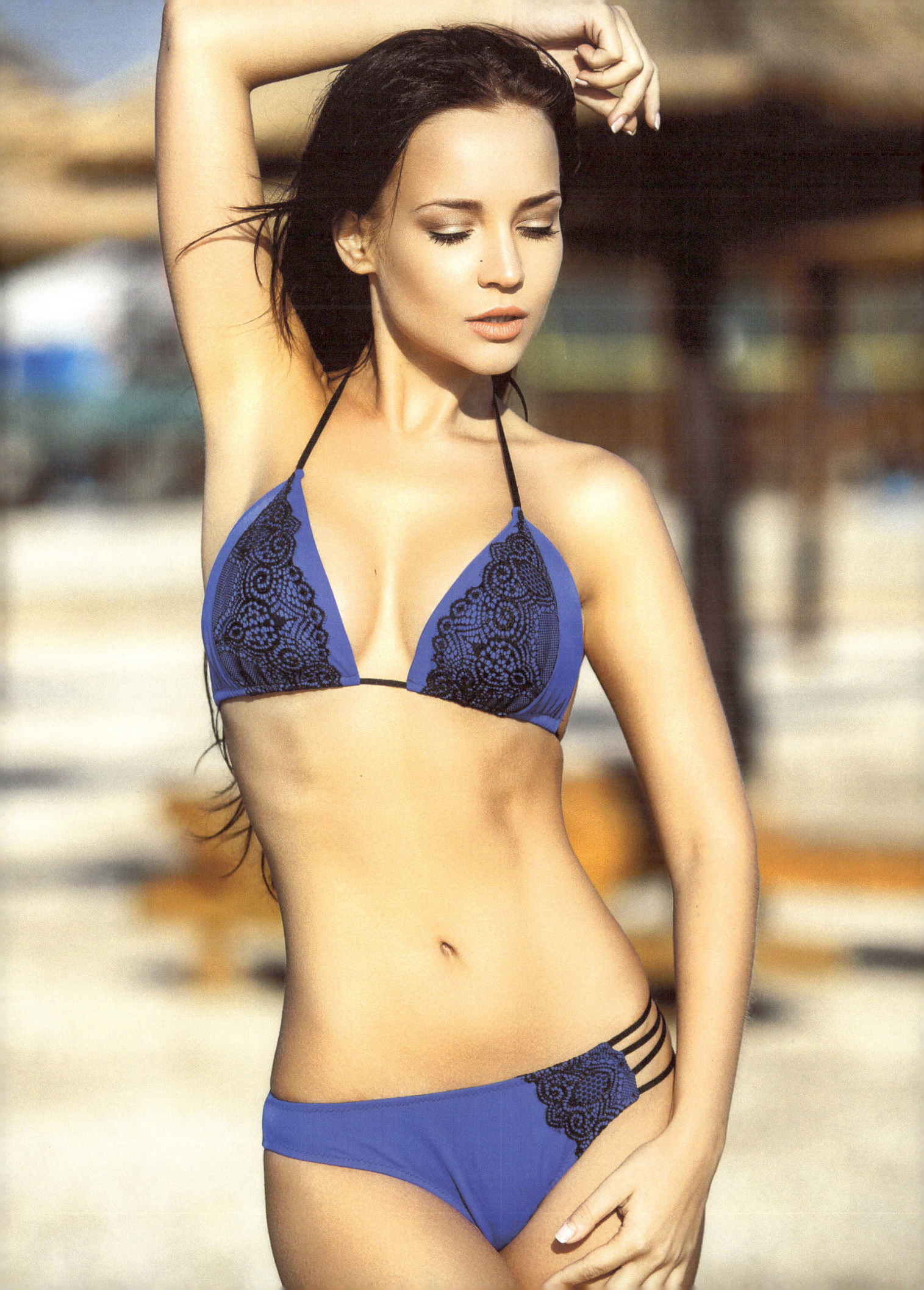

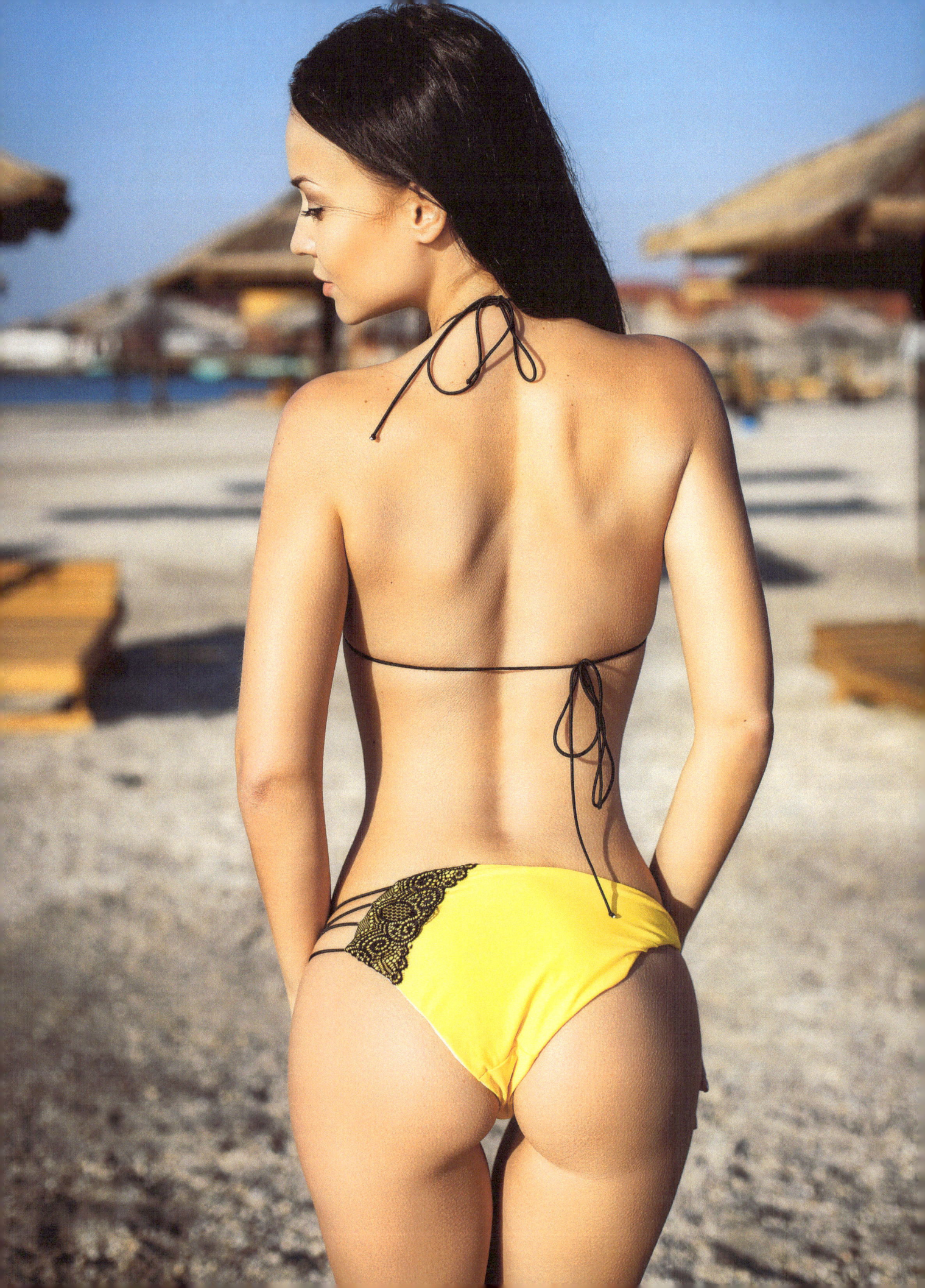

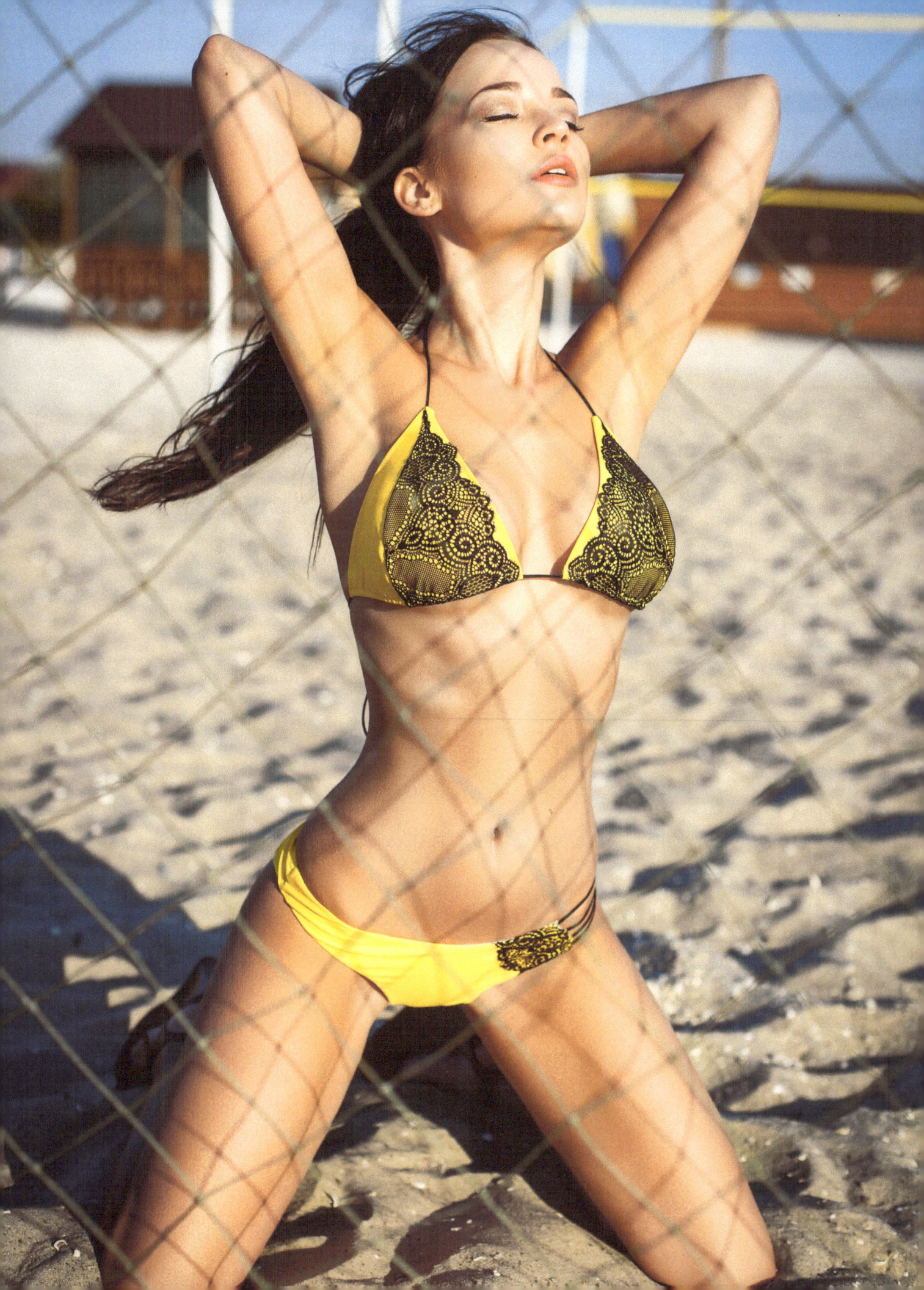

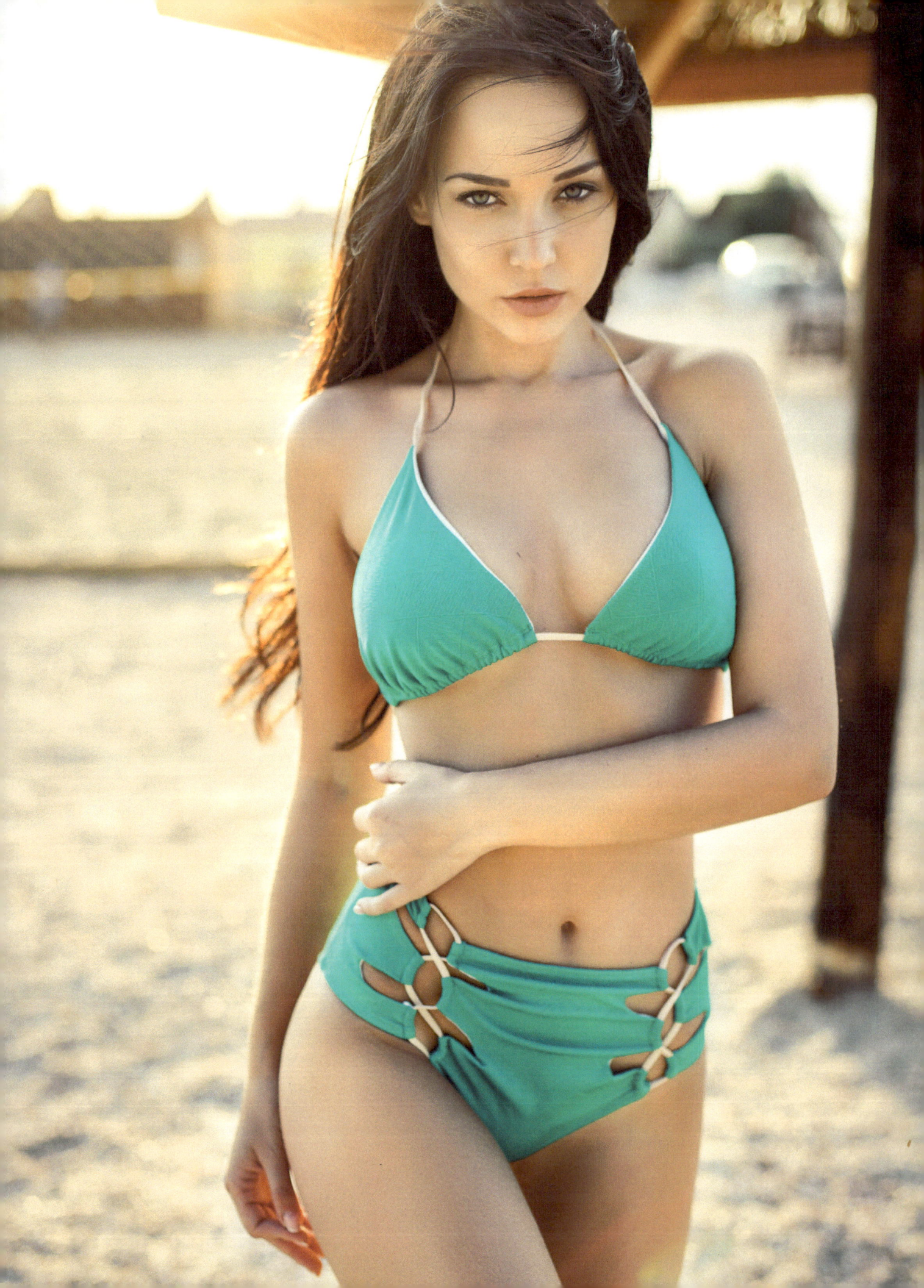

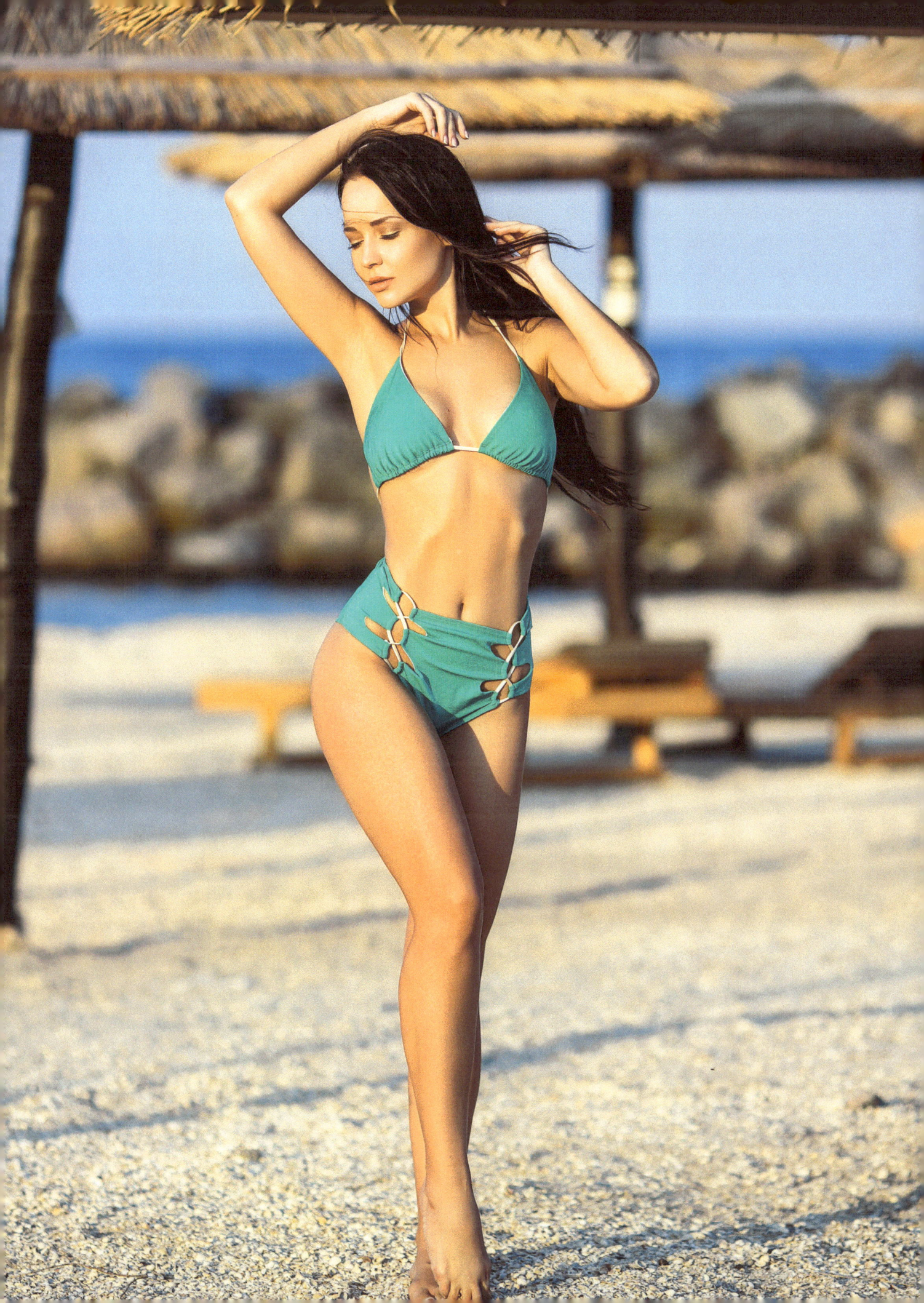

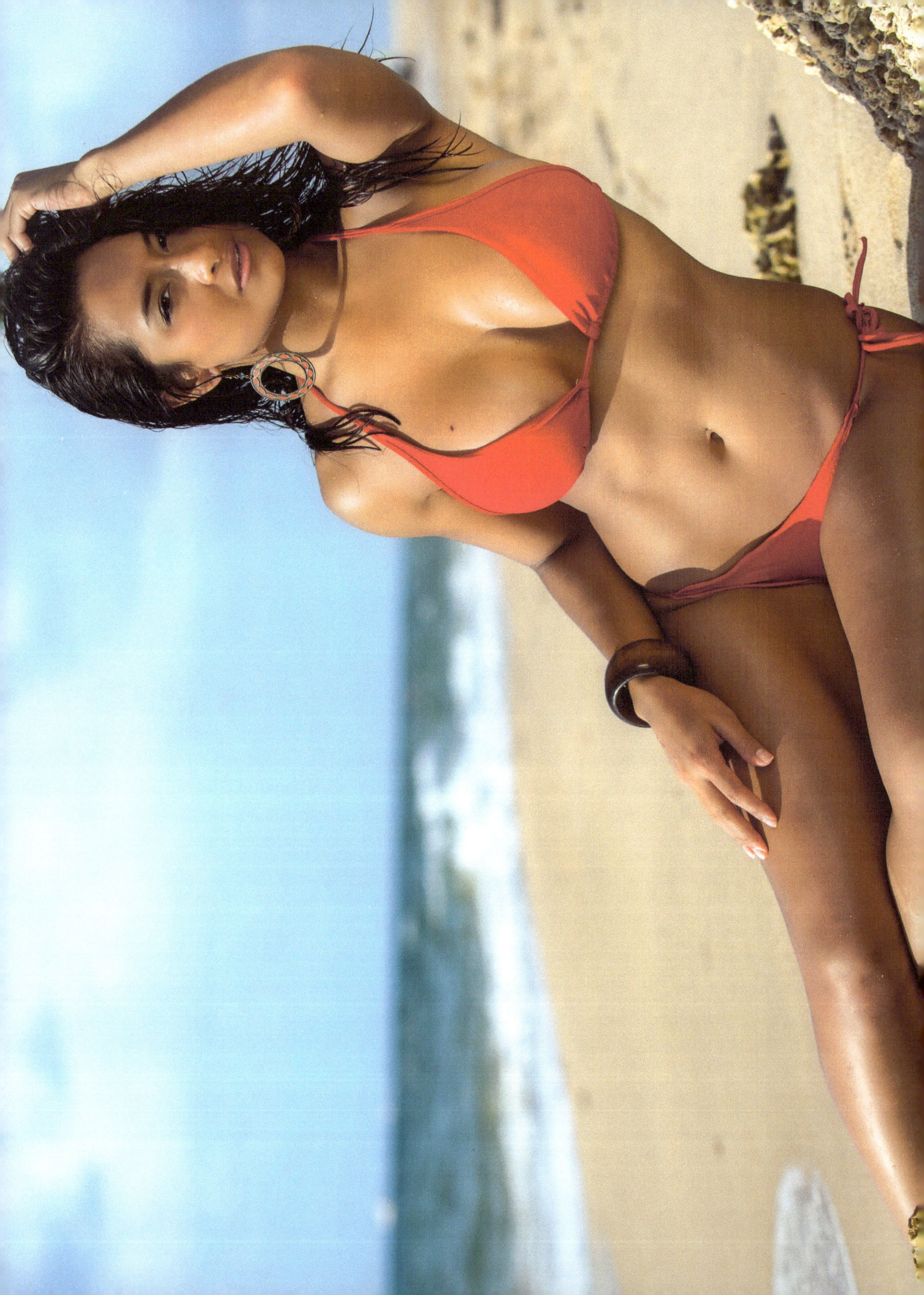

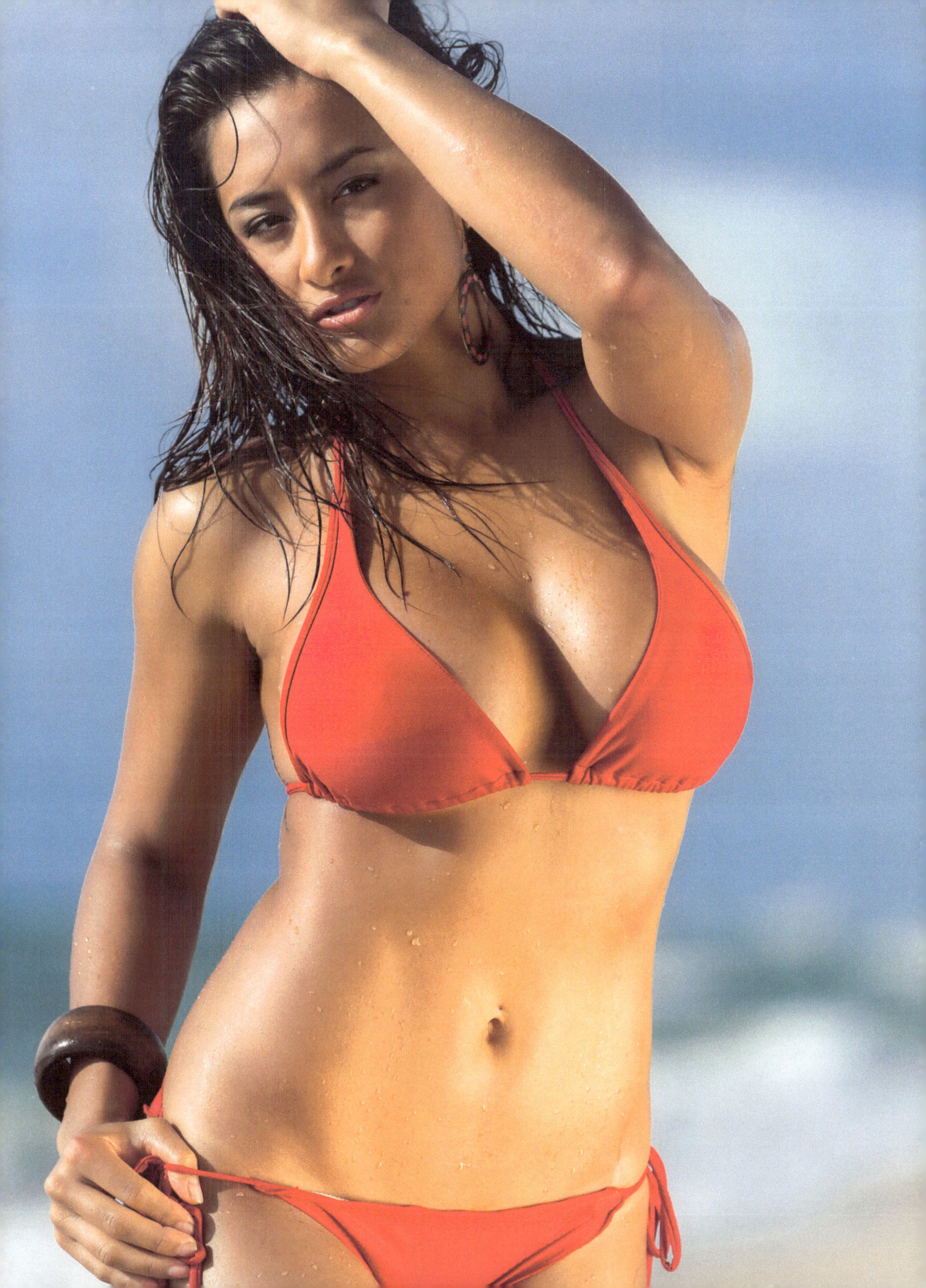

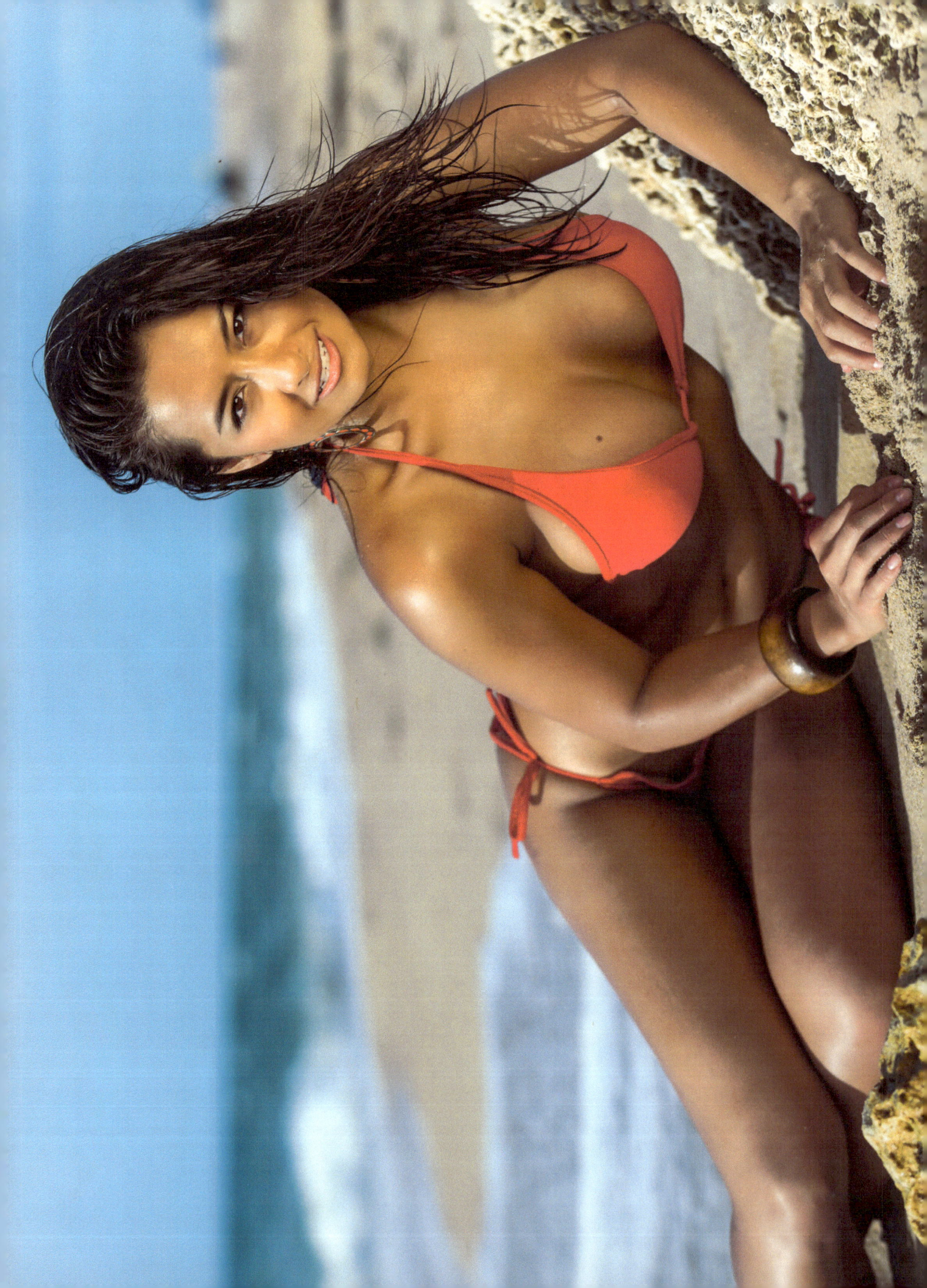

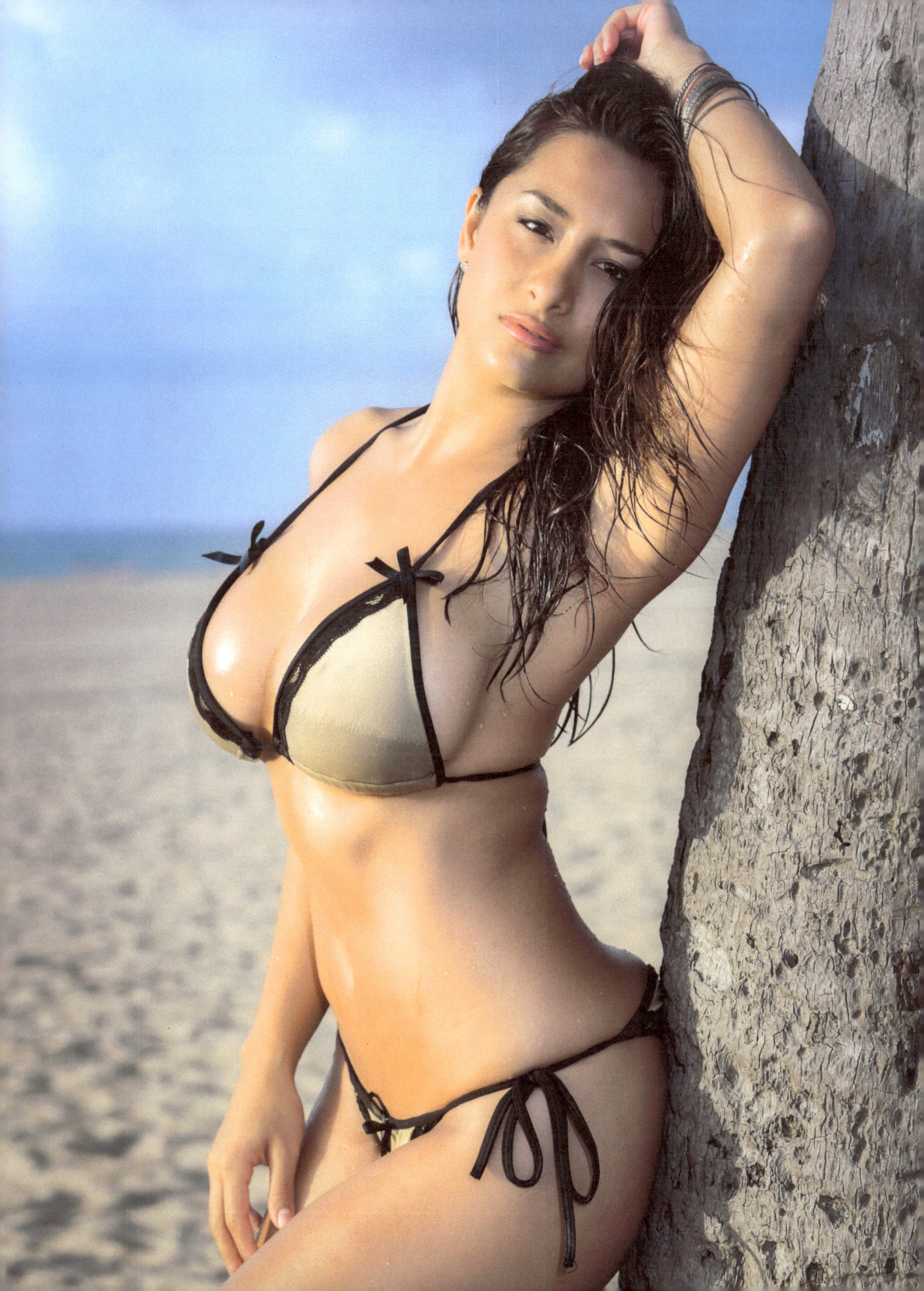

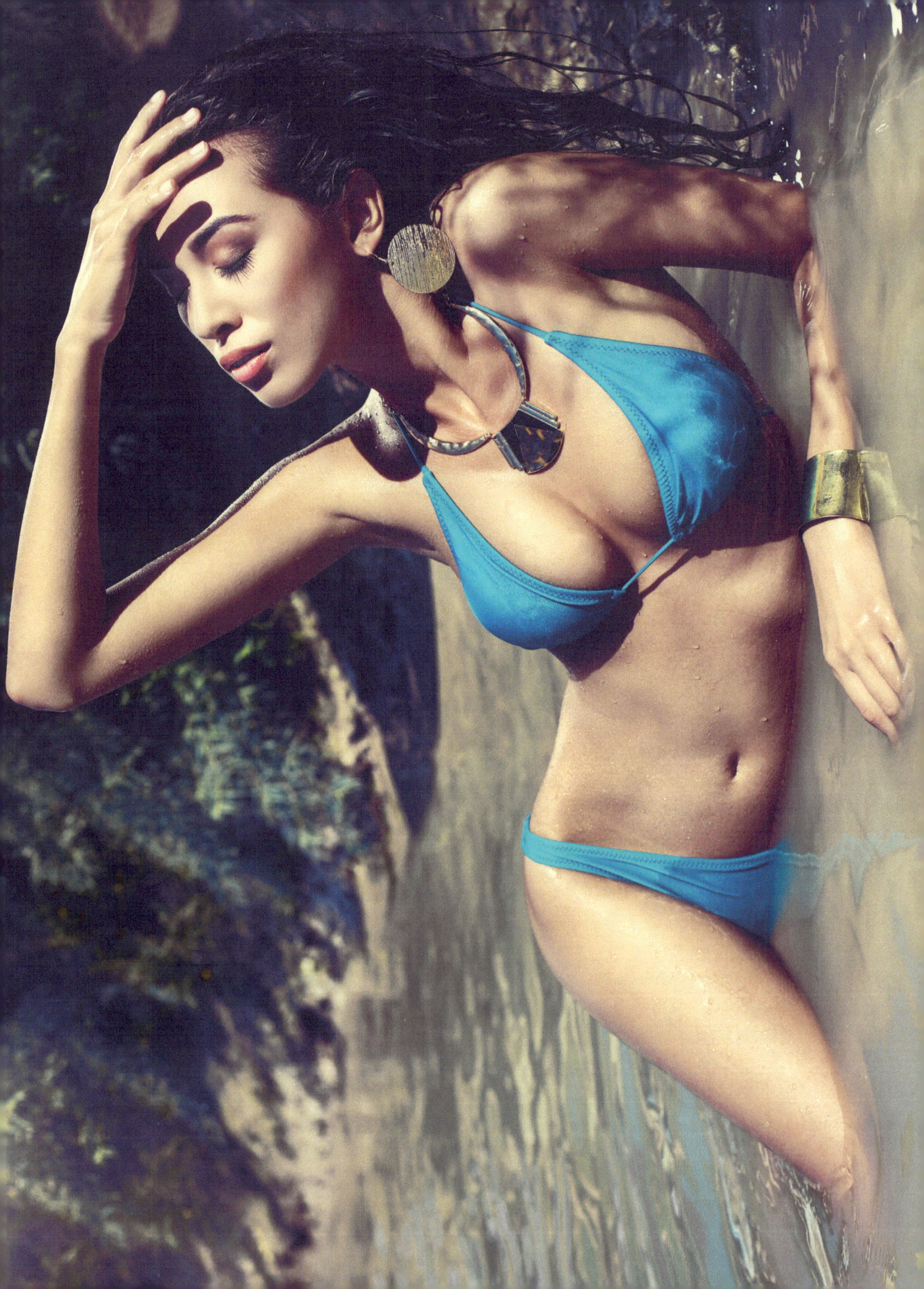

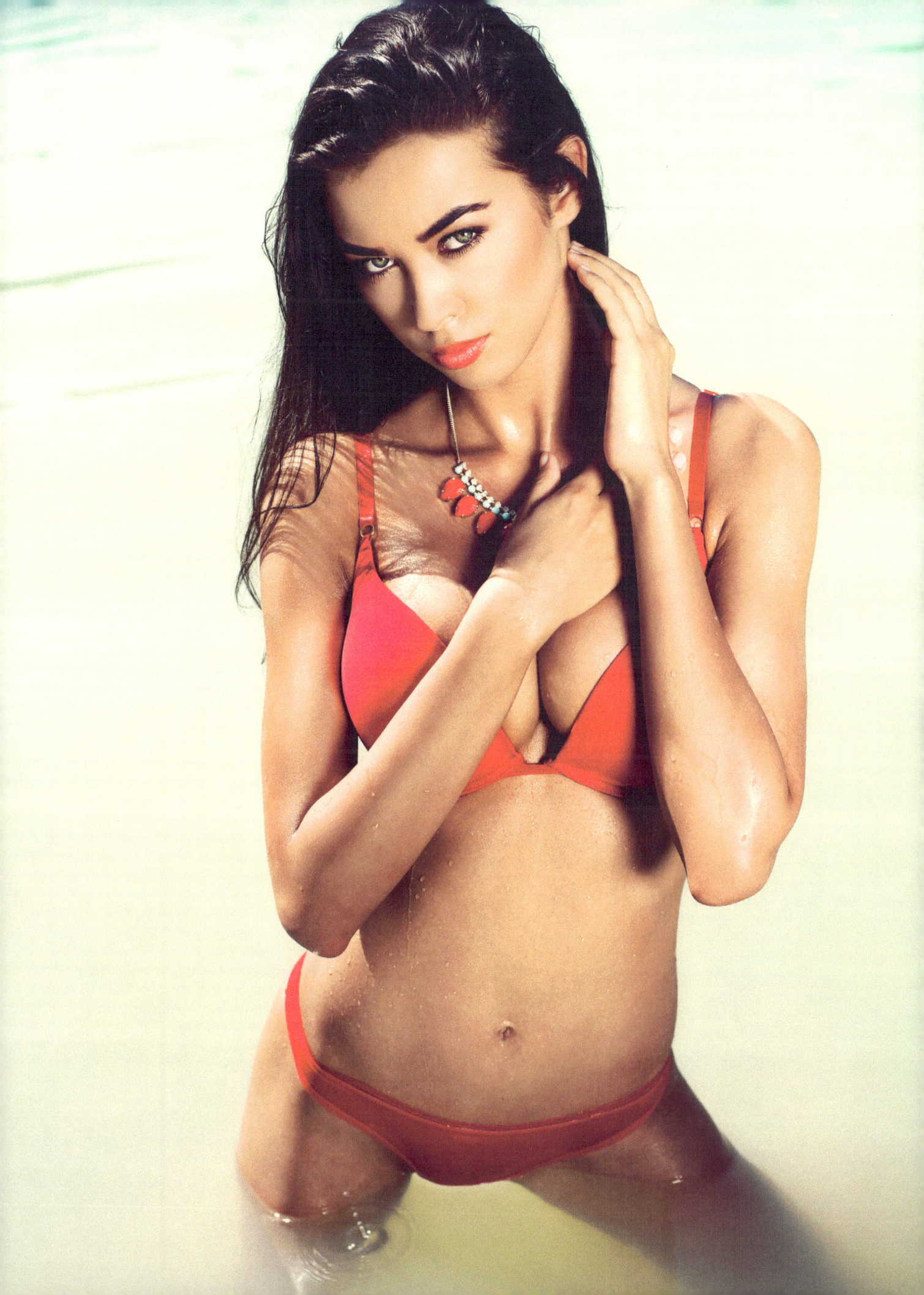

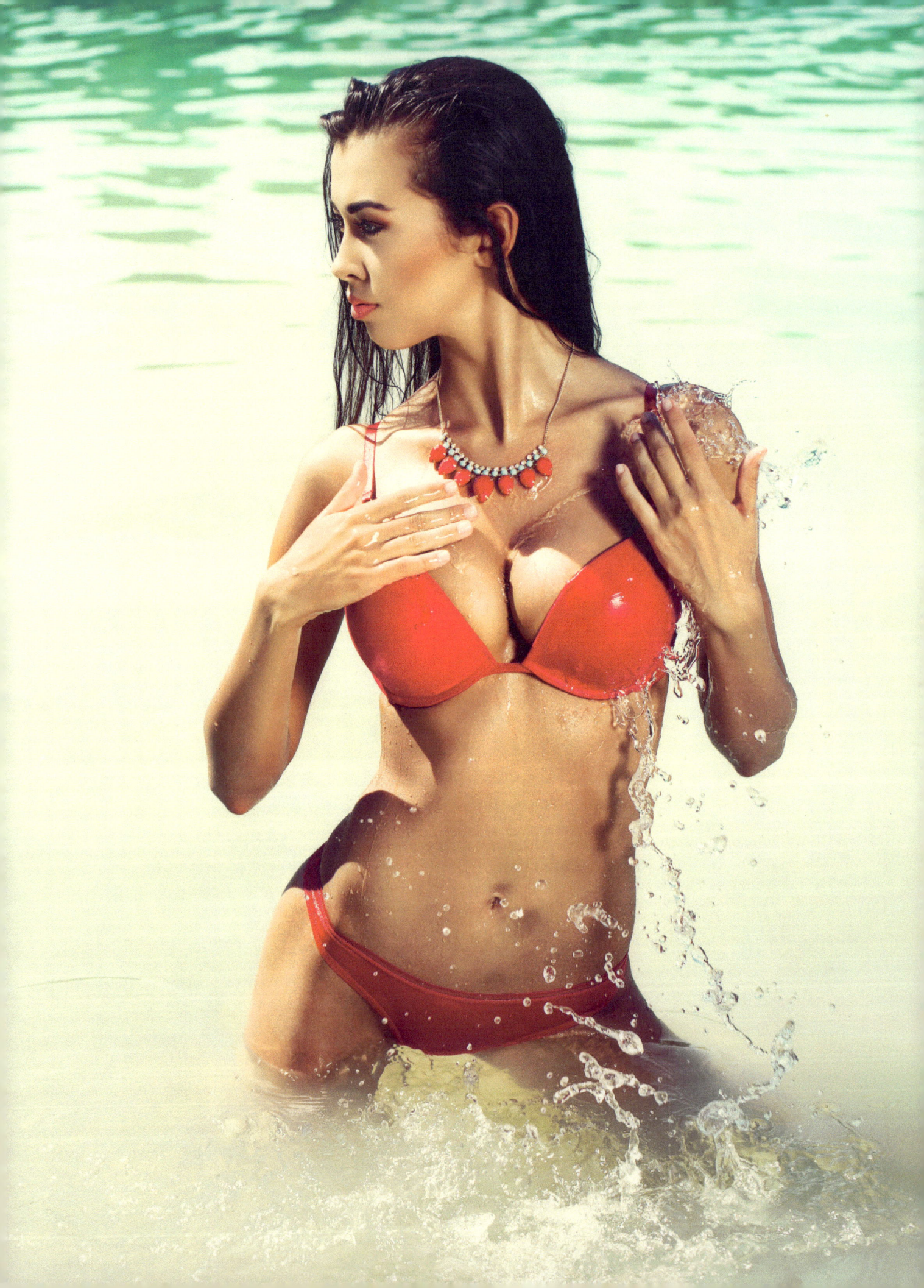

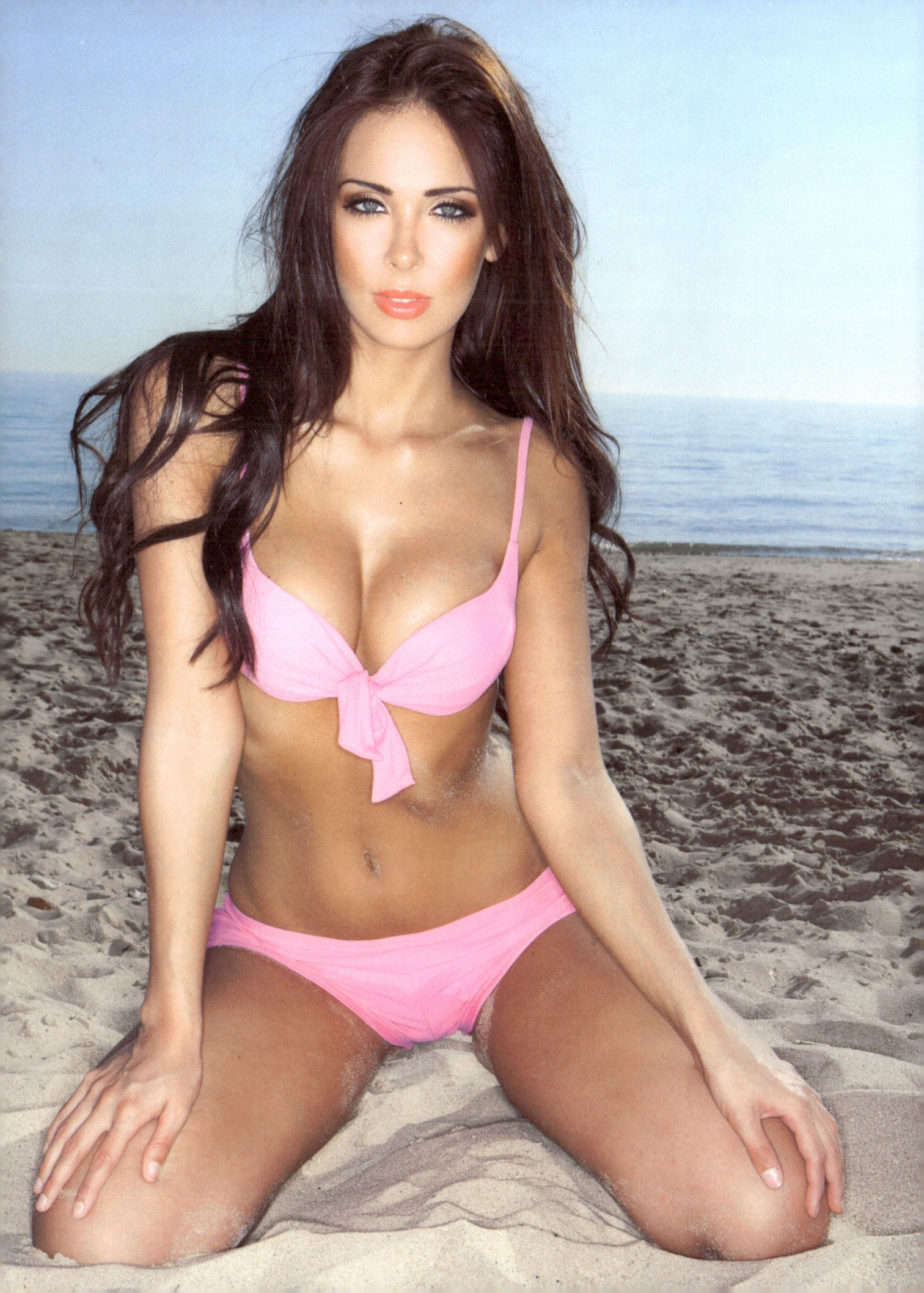

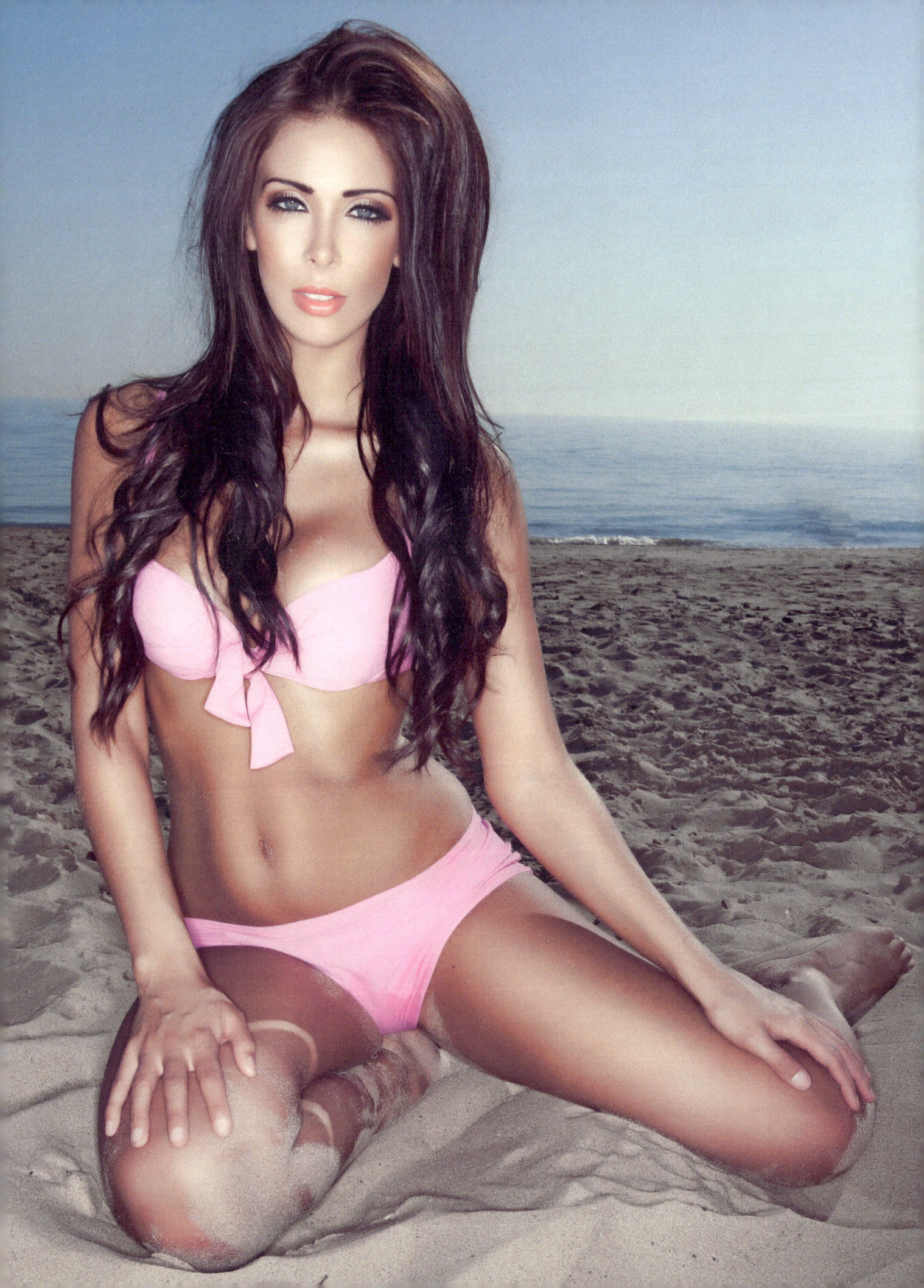

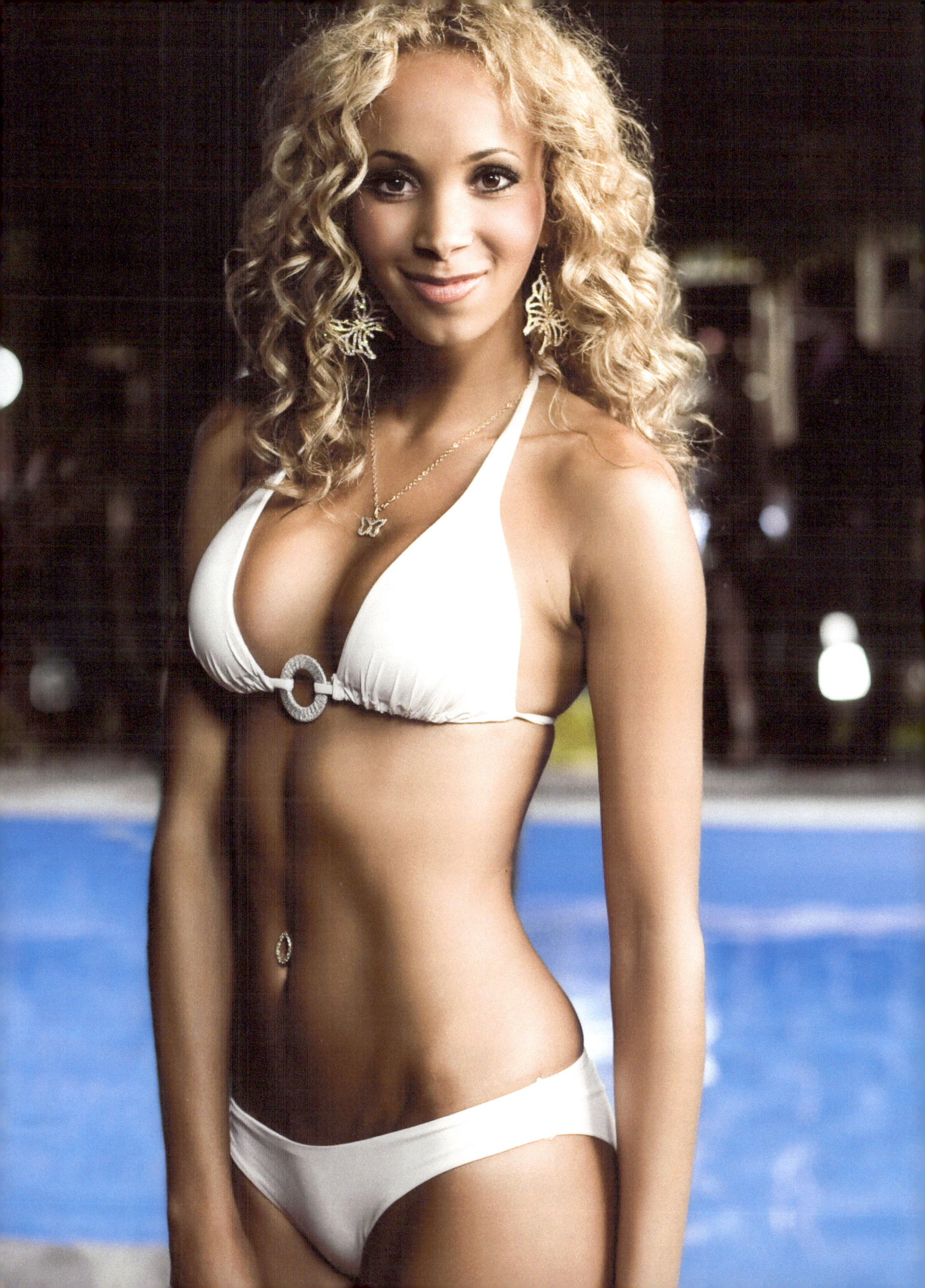

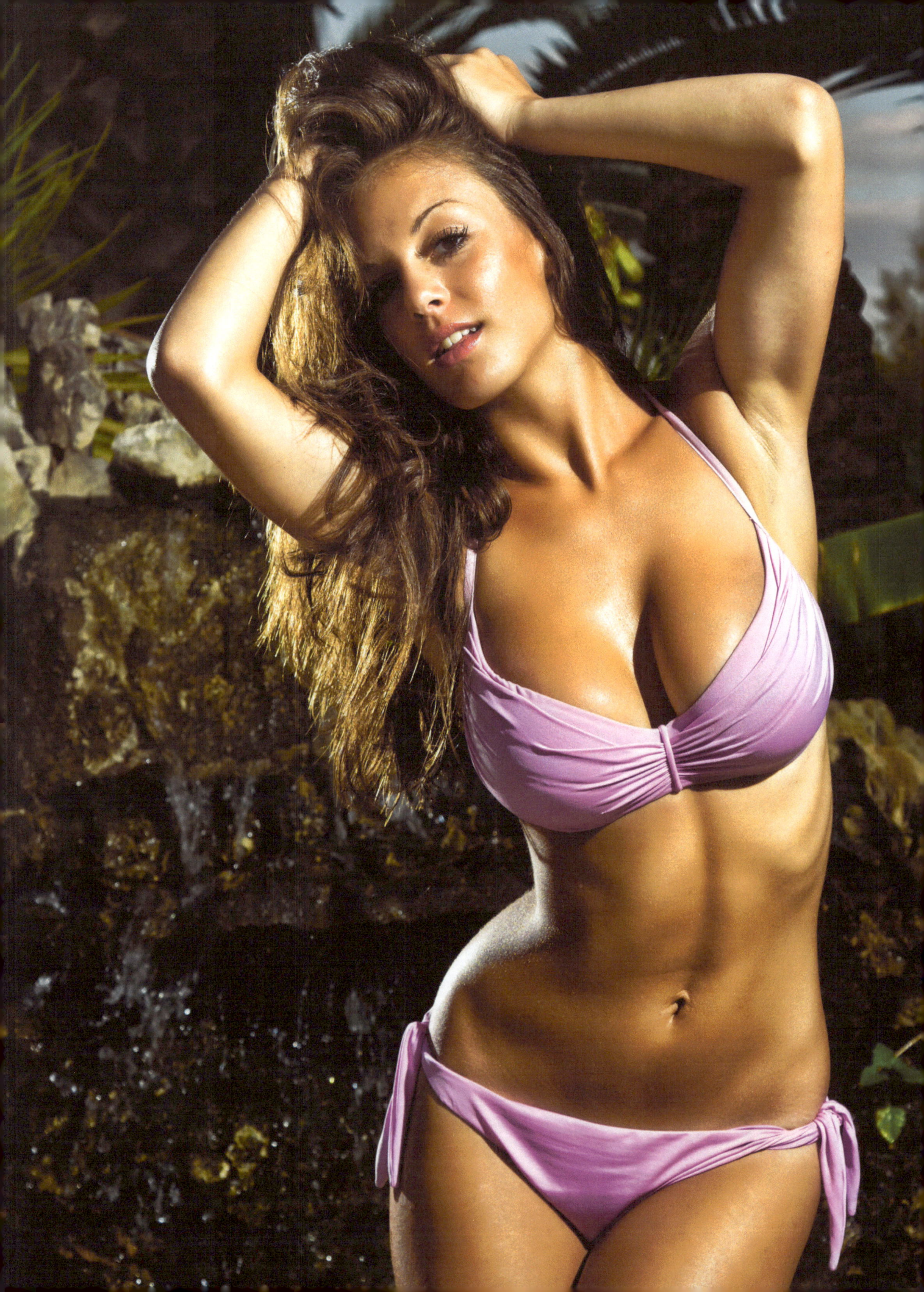

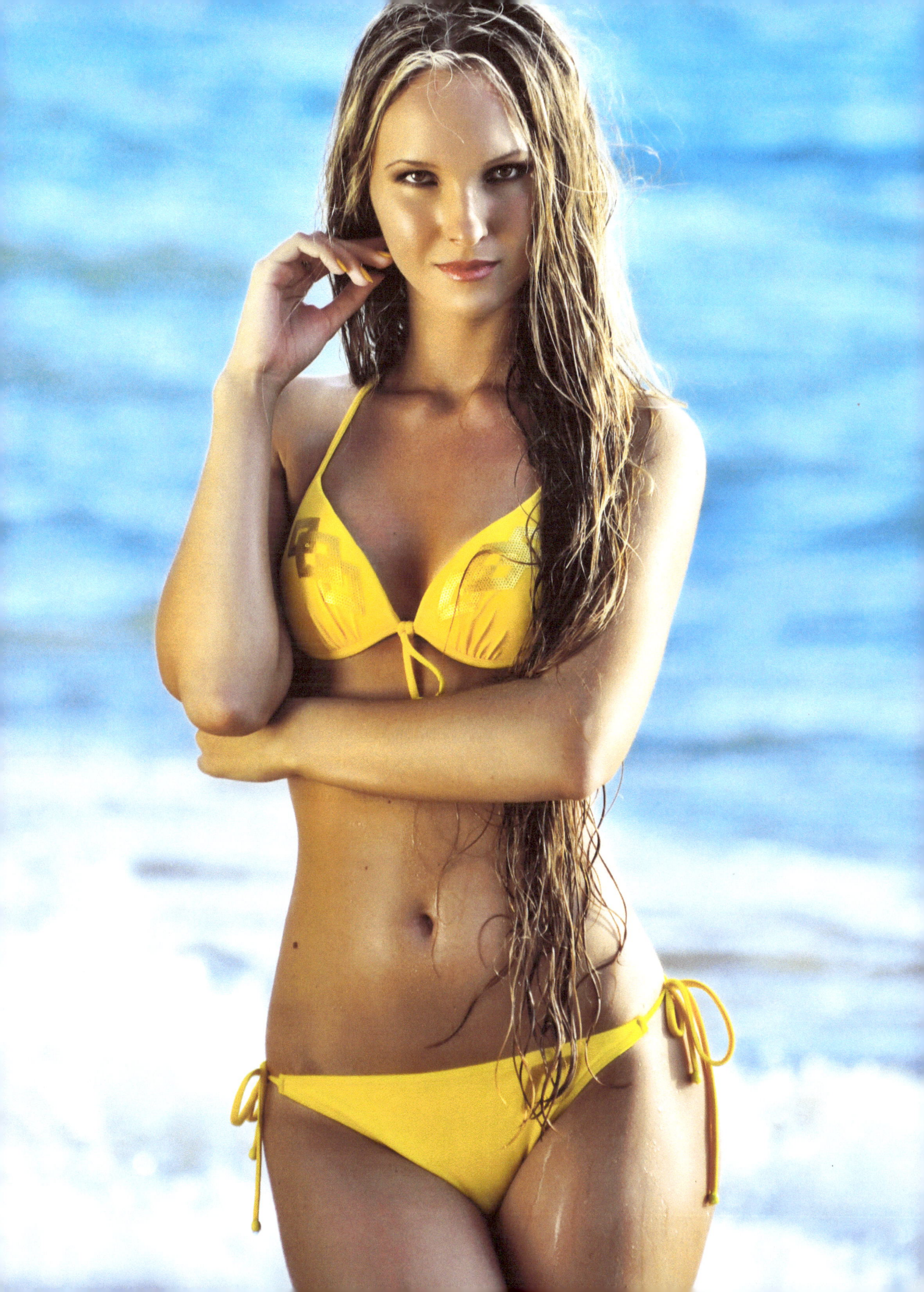

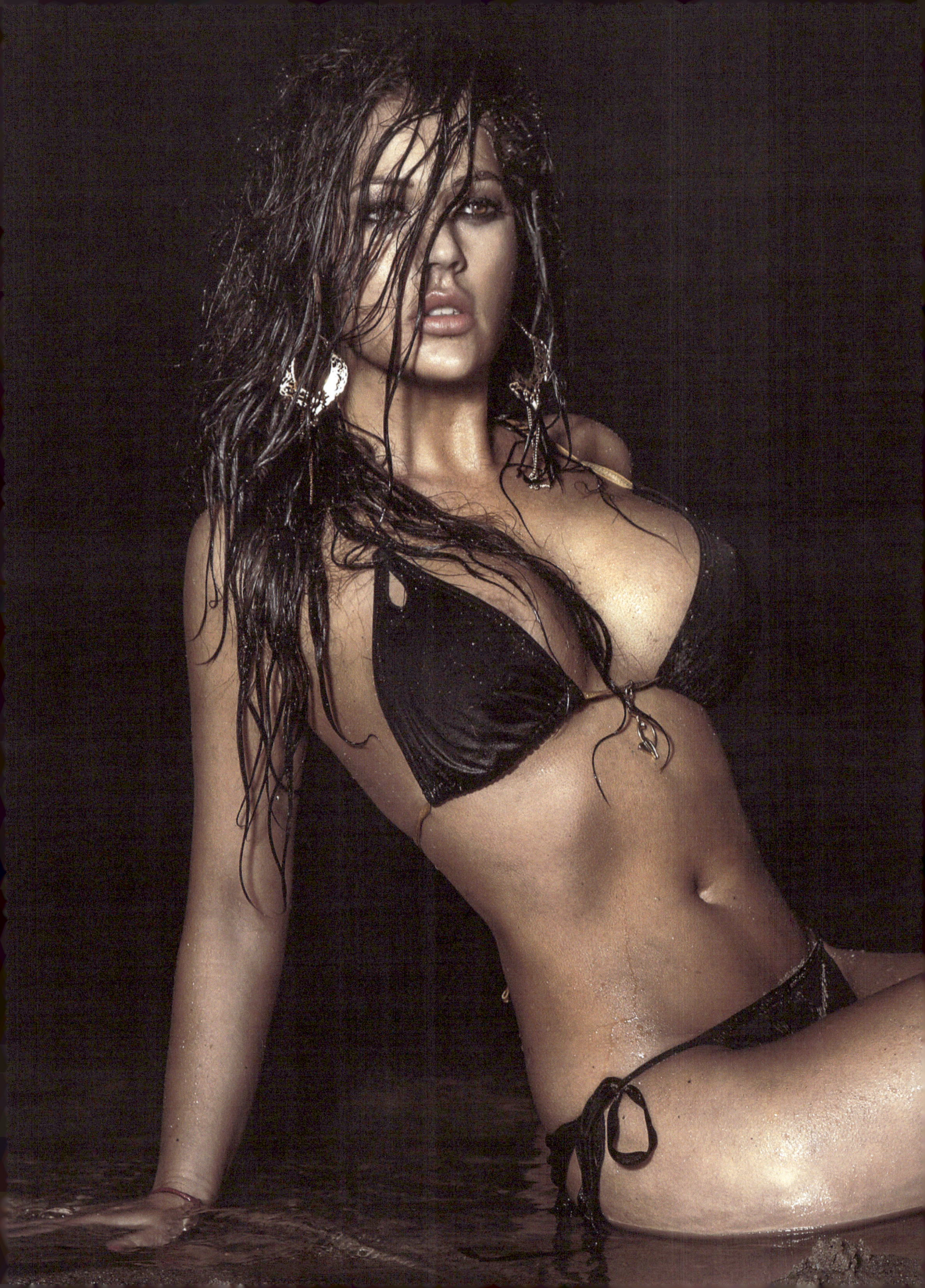

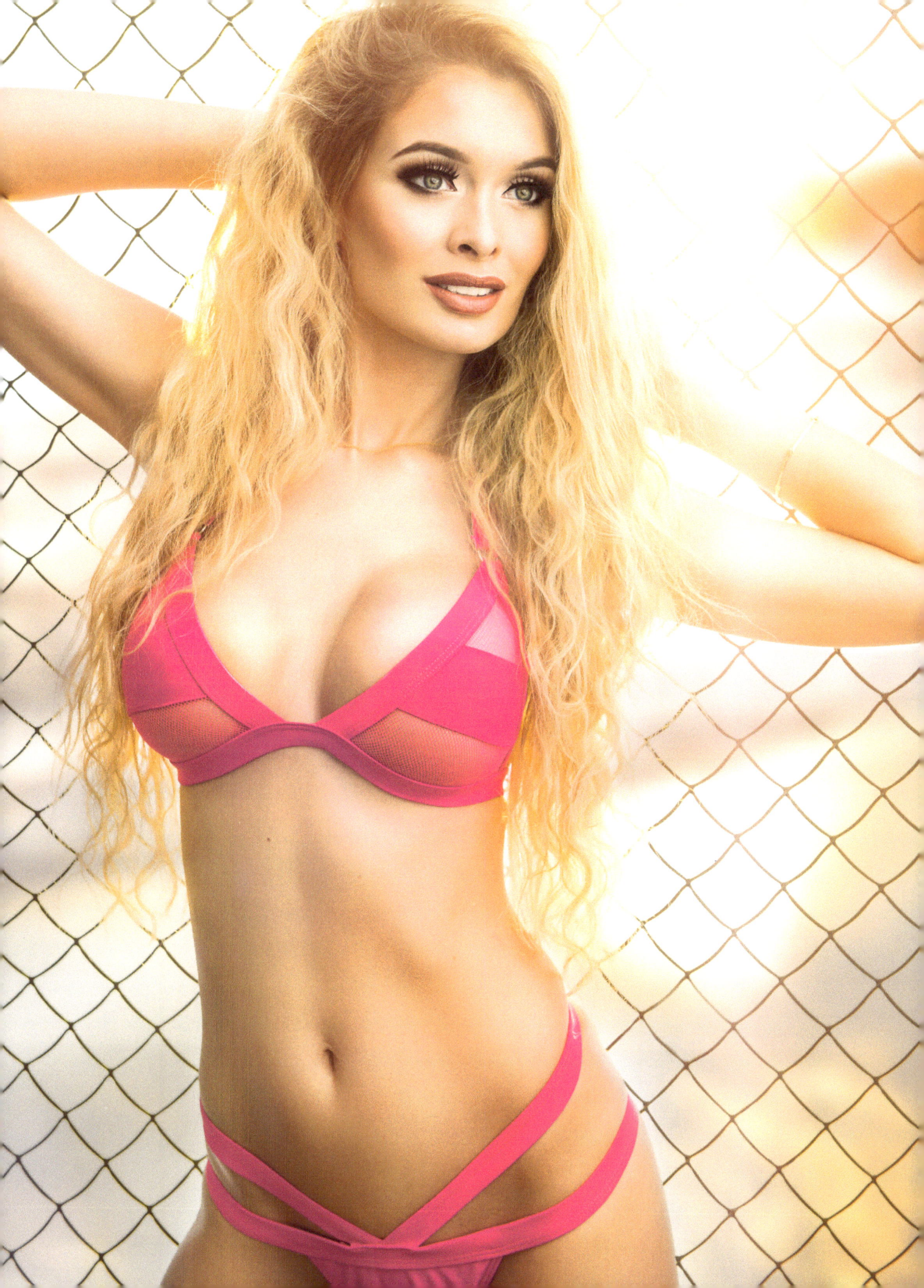

www.ingramcontent.com/pod-product-compliance
Lightning Source LLC
Chambersburg PA
CBHW050417180526
45159CB00005B/2313